ANSWERS to REVISED FIRST AID IN ENGLISH

ISBN 0 7169 4074 4

© Robert Gibson & Sons, 1988

ROBERT GIBSON · **Publisher**
17 Fitzroy Place, Glasgow, G3 7SF

All rights reserved. No part of this publication may be reproduced; stored in a retrieval system; or transmitted in any form or by any means – electronic, mechanical, photocopying, recording, or otherwise – without prior permission of the publisher Robert Gibson & Sons, Ltd., 17 Fitzroy Place, Glasgow, G3 7SF.

Printed by Bell and Bain Ltd., Glasgow

NUMBER

Page 8

1. loaves, men-of-war, pianos, sheep, feet, echoes, pence or pennies, lives, deer, oxen.

2. lady, thief, goose, cloth, trout, passer-by, mouse, knife, tooth, box.

3. armies; sons-in-law; roof; cargoes; woman; child; cupfuls; fly; swine; halos/haloes; dwarfs; potato.

4. (1) We heard the echoes in the caves.
   (2) The ladies spoke to the children.
   (3) The boys went for loaves.
   (4) The men fed the calves.
   (5) The mice ran into holes.
   (6) The knives were lying on the tables.
   (7) The fishermen caught trout.
   (8) The dwarfs gave them sticks.
   (9) The ships struck the reefs.
   (10) Our feet troubled us.
   (11) They were men's boots.
   (12) The burglars tried to rob our shops.
   (13) The prisoners say that they are innocent.
   (14) The girls' hats were on the pegs.
   (15) The boys robbed the birds' nests.
   (16) Their teeth hurt them badly.
   (17) The farmers plough their fields.
   (18) The horses are eating raw carrots.
   (19) The children cried because they were tired.
   (20) These are the houses in which we stay.

5. (1) The rabbits ran from the dogs.
   (2) The girls wore blue dresses.
   (3) The sailors swam to their ships.
   (4) The women caught the geese.
   (5) The men shot the deer.
   (6) The oxen ate the potatoes.
   (7) The ladies preferred the roses.
   (8) The sheep ran in the valleys.
   (9) Their feet were badly cut.
   (10) The thieves stole the valuable bags.
   (11) The children ran to the tables.
   (12) They were men of means.
   (13) We kept the birds in cages.
   (14) They wrote our names.
   (15) The told us so.
   (16) They had sharp knives.
   (17) They took their pencils.
   (18) The old women sat on those seats.
   (19) The men walked slowly to their jobs.
   (20) The mice scampered from the cats.

GENDER

Page 10

1. heiress, nun, mare, niece, goose, waitress, madam, ewe, heroine, spinster.

2. wizard, colt, bull, manservant, husband, drake, bridegroom, fox, duke, uncle.

3.
lion	masculine	cousin	common	jotter	neuter
mistress	feminine	friend	common	pencil	neuter
steward	masculine	sister	feminine	book	neuter
child	common				

3

Gender

Pages 10 – 11

4. lioness; cow; gentleman/lord; grandmother; governor; stag; female; widower; actress; tabby-cat/queen; tailoress; sloven.

5. (1) The bride is my niece.
   (2) The instructress ordered her to jump.
   (3) My landlady is a widow.
   (4) The witch spoke to the princess.
   (5) The cow attacked the milkmaid.
   (6) The Duchess chatted to the woman.
   (7) The heiress to the estate is a spinster.
   (8) "No, madam," she replied.
   (9) The waitress served her own sister.
   (10) "She was indeed a heroine," said the empress.
   (11) The lioness sprang at the filly.
   (12) The mistress gave instructions to the maidservant.
   (13) "Well!" said her grandmother, "How are you, my little lass?"
   (14) The stewardess brought a glass of water to my aunt, who was seasick.
   (15) The conductress of the car directed the famous actress to the theatre.
   (16) The proprietrix of the hotel was a wealthy countess.
   (17) The hostess was extremely puzzled by the twin sisters.
   (18) The daughter of a queen is termed a princess.
   (19) The mayoress talked to the mother of the little girl.
   (20) The old woman told her shepherdess to search for the ewe.

FAMILIES

Page 12

1. cub, eaglet, gosling, lamb, piglet, kid, calf, foal.

2. buck, hind, deer;   dog, bitch;   cob, swan;   cock, hen, fowl;   buck, hare; tom-cat, tabby-cat or queen;   owl;   drake, duck.

3. cub; Nanny-goat, Billy-goat; horse, stallion, mare; cub; piglet; ram, ewe, sheep; gander, goose; eaglet.

4. parr, elver, codling, fry, chick.

HOMES

Page 13

1. caravan, tent, palace, manse, igloo, byre, kennel, eyrie, hive, sty.

2. dove or pigeon, rabbit (tame), sheep, hare, horse.

3. nun, prisoner, American Indian, soldier.

GROUP TERMS OR COLLECTIONS

Page 16

1. choir, fleet, pack, forest, swarm, school, gang, team, litter.
2. animals, rioters, soldiers, rags/papers, stones.
3. fleet, shoal, staff, herd, host, board, bunch, brood, troop, library.
4. pups/cubs, stars/diamonds, musicians, hay, rooks, geese, locusts/insects, sailors, flowers, soldiers.
5. (1) audience; (2) congregation; (3) crowd/throng; (4) mob; (5) rabble; (6) staff.

SIMILES

Page 18

1. a needle/a razor; an eel; a lamb; mustard; a lion; a deer/a hare/a hawk; honey; a bell/crystal; ice/charity; a feather.
2. agile; steady; flat; hard; pleased; clean; tender; timid; busy; old.
3. (1) pancake; (2) rock; (3) deer; (4) peacock; (5) lark.
4. (1) leaf; (2) ice; (3) fish; (4) gold; (5) wind.

OCCUPATIONS

Page 18

Note: There is no ONE correct sentence describing these occupations. The following are merely examples.

The artist paints pictures in water colour or oils.
Athletes train and compete at running, jumping and throwing.
An aviator pilots aeroplanes.
Men go to the barber when they need their hair cut.
The blacksmith shoes horses at his forge.
Housewives buy meat from the butcher.
Much of our furniture is made by a cabinet-maker.
The golfer thanked his caddie for carrying the golf-clubs.
A caretaker looks after flats, houses and other property.
A carpenter uses many wood-working tools in his work.
The cashier has charge of money in a till.
Chauffeurs are employed to drive people in motor cars.
A chemist studies chemicals, and prepares medicines.

Occupations

Pages 18 – 19

A clothier makes and sells clothes.
The circus clown made everyone laugh with his antics.
A coastguard keeps watch for smugglers and ships in distress.
A cobbler works with leather and mends shoes.
Commercial travellers drive many miles to find customers for their goods.
A bus conductor collects passengers' fares.
A confectioner sells sweets.
A decorator paints and papers homes and other buildings, both inside and out.
The dentist extracts teeth and replaces decay with fillings.
Criminals are tracked and traced by detectives.
The doctor gives his patient medical advice and sometimes medicine.
We can buy cloth, cottons and threads from the draper.
A drover moves live animals to and from the market.
An engineer works with machinery of all kinds.
An explorer hopes to discover new places on his travels.
We obtain wheat, barley and similar crops from the farmer.
A farrier shoes horses and looks after them.
A florist sells plants and flowers.
A fruiterer sells fruit and vegetables.
A gamekeeper protects wild animals and birds on an estate from being caught or killed unlawfully.
A glazier puts glass in windows.
The greengrocer keeps a variety of fruit and vegetables in his shop.
Today I bought coffee, tea, butter and jam from the grocer.
A hosier sells socks and stockings.
The ironmonger sells tools, pots, pans, nails and screws.
A jockey rides horses in races.
A joiner works with wood, usually making smaller items than those made by a carpenter.
A journalist writes for newspapers and magazines.
The judge hears evidence and passes sentence on criminals in court.
A lawyer studies the law and represents others in a court of law.
The locksmith makes locks and keys.
A magistrate administers the law in local courts.
A mason builds and works with stone and brick.
The matron of the hospital was very strict with all nurses who worked under her.
The mechanic looks after machinery and does repairs.
A milliner makes and sells hats for ladies.

Occupations

Pages 18 – 19

<u>Miners</u> dig underground for coal and other minerals.
A <u>minister</u> conducts services in a church.
A <u>navvy</u> is an unskilled labourer engaged on construction works, originally canals (navigations) in particular.
A <u>newsagent's</u> shop is usually full of newspapers and magazines.
A <u>nurse</u> usually works in a hospital and looks after sick and injured people.
An <u>optician</u> tests eyes and makes and sells spectacles.
A <u>pedlar</u> goes from door to door selling small household goods from a pack or suitcase.
A <u>poacher</u> secretly looks for and kills animals and birds on private estates, and usually sells them unlawfully.
A <u>policeman</u> has to protect life and property and can arrest anyone breaking the law.
Some <u>porters</u> are doorkeepers, others carry loads in markets or warehouses, or luggage in railway stations.
A <u>postman</u> delivers letters and parcels.
Our <u>plumber</u> repaired our burst water pipes and also checked the gas pipes.
A <u>saddler</u> makes leather goods, particularly saddles and harness.
A <u>sailor</u> works on a ship as a member of the crew.
A <u>sawyer's</u> work is sawing and cutting timber.
The bronze, marble and wooden statues in the palace were the work of famous <u>sculptors</u>.
The <u>seamstress</u> worked hard to finish sewing the dress in time.
The old <u>shepherd</u> never tired of looking after his sheep on the hills.
A <u>slater</u> works on roofs with slates.
The <u>soldier</u> had been in the army for many years and had fought in several battles.
A <u>stationer</u> sells paper, pens, ink and other writing materials.
A <u>steeplejack</u> works at great heights, mending steeples and tall chimneys.
A <u>stoker</u> feeds the fires in furnaces or boilers with fuel.
A <u>surgeon</u> is a doctor who treats injuries and diseases by means of amputations and other operations.
The <u>tailor</u> makes clothes, particularly suits for men.
A <u>teacher</u> tries to pass on knowledge and skills to children and other students.
We had a leaking pot and a kettle mended by the <u>tinker</u>.
The <u>tinsmith</u> makes articles of tin or tin-plate.
A <u>tourist</u> travels from place to place on holiday, interested in seeing as much as possible.
A <u>witness</u> is a person who has seen something happen, and in a law-court gives evidence about something he has seen or knows about.
A <u>wright</u> is a maker of something, as in "wheelwright" or "playwright".

Occupations

Page 19

Associations

blacksmith	glazier	postman	soldier	optician
cobbler	tourist	witness	slater	astronomer
gardener/ street trader	soldier	pedlar	miner	seamstress
orchestra conductor/ policeman	policeman	artist	carpenter/ joiner	conductor (bus)
businessman	saddler	carpenter	butcher/grocer/ greengrocer/ shopkeeper	musician
farmer	milliner	farmer/ ploughman	shepherd	policeman
butcher	airman	chemist	navvy/stoker	nurse
surgeon	butcher/cutler	clergyman	tinker/plumber	judge/advocate/ barrister
stoker	surgeon	barber	mechanic	

Chief Persons

general/ field-marshall	superintendent/ matron	superintendent/ inspector	headmaster/ headmistress
principal	admiral	postmaster	captain
chairman	editor	governor	captain
judge	conductor	stationmaster	foreman/overseer

PLACES

Page 19

Business

Places where made:
   brewery, bakery, studio, mill, foundry, tannery, mint, paper-mill, shipyard, distillery.

Particular shops:
   baker, clothier, tailor, outfitter/draper, fishmonger, florist, fruiterer/greengrocer, grocer, milliner/hatter, butcher, dairy, newsagent, poulterer, optician, hosier, confectioner, tobacconist, greengrocer, stationer,

Sport

court, green, ring, pitch/ground, lawn, pitch/field/ground, course, pitch/field/, green, pitch/ground, track/stadium, rink, run, court, ring.

Places

Page 19

General

hangar, apiary/hive, aviary, bullring, incubator, kitchen, gaol/prison, rookery, museum, law-court, garage, theatre, orphanage, cemetery, restaurant, theatre.

Page 20

surgery, cinema, aquarium, orchard, gas-holder/gasometer, granary, vineyard, school, barracks, reservoir, zoo, nursery, nursery.

Differences

Yacht	— a vessel, using wind and sails, for pleasure cruising or racing, usually privately owned.
Ferry	— a boat used for conveying people or things across a (usually) short stretch of water for payment.
Motor	— provides road transport.
Aeroplane	— provides air transport.
River	— is a natural waterway.
Canal	— is a man-made waterway.
Pen	— a writing tool for which ink is needed.
Pencil	— a writing tool using "lead" (graphite) embedded within it.
Shoes	— footwear not covering the ankles.
Boots	— footwear covering the ankles.
Chair	— a seat for one person.
Sofa	— a seat for two or more persons.
Pin	— pierces and holds together two or more pieces of material or paper.
Needle	— is used for joining material with thread, held in its eye, and pulled through the material after the needle.
Tramcar	— runs on rails, and is usually powered by electricity.
Omnibus	— is steered by the driver, and usually powered by oil or petrol.
Shadow	— a dark area cast by an object obstructing light.
Reflection	— an image sent back from a mirror or other polished surface.
Clock	— large timepiece placed on a table, mantelshelf, wall or tower.
Watch	— small timepiece worn on the wrist or carried in the pocket.
Ham	— pig's flesh from the thigh.
Bacon	— pig's flesh from back or sides.
Hay	— grass dried for fodder.
Straw	— cut stalks of corn plants.

RECEPTACLES

Page 20

Contents

documents, hats/collars, wine/spirits/beer/oil/tar, water, fruit/groceries, water, rubbish, water, liquid, fruit/soup/porridge, tools/sweets, documents, coal, wine/beer, tea, fruit/vegetables, tea/shot, wine, wine, bottles, face powder, fish, condiments, tea/coffee, crockery/clothes, wine/spirits, oil, letter, water, cider, tea/spirits, watch, gas, wine, tennis racket, food, money/personal belongings, wine, marmalade/jam, milk/water, beer/gunpowder, water, uniform (soldier's), books, biscuits, food being cooked, water, medicine, banknotes, drawings/certificates, stew/seedling plant, strawberries, money, money/valuables, school books, sword, coal, whisky, water/petrol, beer, tea, hot drink, money, clothes, ice-cream/water, water, beer/wine, tea/ashes of the dead, flowers, liquids, paper money/documents, clothes.

Receptacles and Containers

purse/wallet, reservoir/bowl/tank, bottle/sauce-boat, jar, scuttle, band-box/hat-box, scabbard, vase.

FASTENINGS

Page 20

door, trousers, door/gate, trousers, dress/kilt, shirt/blouse/dress, ship (anchor), bricks, anchor, paper, dressing gown, rails (railway), wood/rubber/leather/paper, paper/stamp/envelope, wrists, horse and cart, ship, door, clothes, shoe/boot, window/door, door/safe/suitcase, bricks/stonework, wood, gate/box, wallpaper, tent ropes, cloth, window glass, metal plates, sail, metal, paper/fencing, bag/attaché case, parcel, wings of aircraft, floor coverings, pieces of cloth, parcel, clothes.

SOUNDS AND MOTIONS

Page 22

1. brays; trumpets; neighs; grunts; howls; chatters; bells; lows; growls; screams.

2. The <u>hound</u> bays.　　　　　　The <u>frog</u> croaks.
   The <u>snake</u> hisses.　　　　　 The <u>cat</u> purrs.
   The <u>cock</u> crows.　　　　　　The <u>turkey</u> gobbles.
   The <u>lamb</u> bleats.　　　　　　The <u>lion</u> roars.
   The <u>crow</u> caws.　　　　　　 The <u>duck</u> quacks.

3. The frog <u>leaps</u>.　　　　　　The duck <u>waddles</u>.
   The monkey <u>climbs</u>.　　　　The lamb <u>frisks</u>.
   The wolf <u>lopes</u>.　　　　　　The lark <u>soars</u>.
   The seagull <u>swoops/glides</u>.　The bear <u>lumbers</u>.

Sounds and Motions

Pages 22 – 23

4. The <u>obstinate</u> mule.   The <u>cunning</u> fox.
   The <u>fat</u> pig.   The <u>gentle</u> lamb.
   The <u>faithful</u> dog.   The <u>sleek</u> cat.
   The <u>loathsome</u> serpent.   The <u>tireless</u> seagull.

5. (1) bull, (2) camel, (3) bee/wasp, (4) cock, (5) dog, (6) frog, (7) pig, (8) monkey, (9) horse, (10) wolf, (11) hen, (12) bee, (13) parrot, (14) horse, (15) hyena/wolf/dog, (16) owl.

6. (1) aquiline — (a nose) hooked like an eagle's beak.
   (2) feline — (walked) silently like a cat.
   (3) bovine — resembling a cow or an ox.
   (4) asinine — stupid (behaviour) like that of an ass.
   (5) canine — (teeth) like those of a dog.

7. (1) an ape — a person of ungainly behaviour or appearance/or a copier.
   (2) an ass — a stupid person.
   (3) a bear — large, lumbering and clumsy.
   (4) a bull — someone who angrily insists on getting his own way.
   (5) a dog — a scoundrel.
   (6) a donkey — a stupid obstinate person.
   (7) an elephant — a ponderous clumsy person.
   (8) a fox — someone who is cunning in his dealing with others.
   (9) a goat — someone who behaves foolishly.
   (10) a horse — someone willing to burden himself with problems and/or tasks of others, a hard worker.
   (11) a hound — a despicable person.
   (12) a lamb — someone meek and placid in nature.
   (13) a lion — a courageous person, a much admired leader.
   (14) a pig — a dirty, greedy, bad-mannered person.
   (15) a rabbit — timid, nervous person.
   (16) a sheep — someone who will follow the crowd rather than act as an individual.
   (17) a snail — a slow-moving, slow-thinking person.
   (18) a swine — a coarse unscrupulous person.
   (19) a tortoise — a slow-moving person.
   (20) a viper — someone who is spiteful and treacherous.

SOUNDS (Made by Objects)

Page 23

1. The <u>creak</u> of a hinge.   The <u>crack</u> of a whip.
   The <u>screeching</u> of brakes.   The <u>hissing</u> of steam.
   The <u>patter</u> or <u>tramp</u> of feet.   The <u>rustle</u> of silk.
   The <u>call</u> of a bugle.   The <u>tick</u> of a clock.

SOUNDS (Made by Objects)

Page 24

2. The pealing of <u>bells</u>. The popping of <u>corks</u>.
   The booming of <u>guns</u>. The skirl of the <u>pipes</u>.
   The crinkle of <u>paper</u>. The throb of an <u>engine</u>.
   The slam of a <u>door</u>. The toot of a <u>horn</u>.

3. A boiling kettle <u>whistles</u>. Thunder <u>rumbles</u>. Frying fat <u>sizzles</u> in the pan. The rain <u>patters</u> on the window. Coins <u>jingle</u> in the bag. I heard the <u>report</u> of a rifle. The heavy bar fell with a <u>crash/thud</u>. Suddenly we heard the <u>clatter</u> of hoofs.

CLASSIFICATION

Pages 24 – 25

(1) cauliflower	(7) scone	(13) heat	(19) maize	(25) calico
(2) hare	(8) whale	(14) milk	(20) princess	(26) wagon
(3) violet	(9) pearl	(15) shield	(21) palm	(27) fork
(4) slate	(10) Glasgow	(16) liner	(22) Jane	(28) radiator
(5) lemon	(11) Spain	(17) warehouse	(23) cupboard	(29) London
(6) cement	(12) biscuit	(18) tomatoes	(24) potato	(30) crocodile

Page 25

(1) turban	(6) iron	(11) zinc	(16) heron	(21) lily
(2) bowl	(7) trout	(12) fly	(17) blouse	(22) soup
(3) owl	(8) sofa	(13) Nairobi	(18) bicycle	(23) guitar
(4) rose	(9) skunk	(14) trawler	(19) eel	(24) beetroot
(5) ear	(10) peach	(15) toffee	(20) cricket	(25) milliner

ANALOGIES

Page 26

1. mouse
2. pork
3. platform
4. man
5. April
6. up
7. South
8. nephew
9. army
10. bray
11. finger
12. feathers
13. pleasure/happiness/joy
14. leg
15. gross
16. bullet
17. dog
18. hoof
19. son
20. picture
21. ice
22. swan
23. shoal
24. bee
25. fish
26. modern
27. double
28. herd
29. this
30. month
31. ate
32. can
33. hot water
34. pig
35. hot
36. water

DOUBLES

Page 27

1. lock and key
2. spick and span
3. again and again
4. odds and ends
5. puff and blow

ABBREVIATIONS

Page 30

1. 'tis, needn't, you'll, Hallowe'en, sou'wester, I've, 'twas, ne'er, o'clock, don't.
2. Justice of the Peace, British Broadcasting Corporation, Cash on delivery, Member of Parliament/Military Police, General Post Office, Before Christ, Master of Arts, His/Her Royal Highness, Leg before wicket, British Rail.
3. *ante meridiem* — before noon, instant — this month, *proximo* — next month, *ultimo* — last month, Esquire, Road, Mister, Weather permitting, *post meridiem* — after noon, Street.

OPPOSITES

Page 30

1.
home	white	deny	sober	true
presence	curse	expand	wet	unfamiliar
refuse	timid	incorrect	bright	unknown
child	top	hero	giant	simple/plain
dead	stern	bless	late	near
descendant	dull	dry	west	thin
modern	narrow	light	difficult	strong
question	sell	night	flow	barren
depart	free	victory	uneducated	many
awake	freedom	attack	full	last
disperse/dismantle	expensive/dear	shallow	friend/ally	ebb
front	slim	admit	exit	friend/ally
forward	dirty	arrive	morning	wise
good	stupid	height	never	native
fertile	smooth	live	nowhere	lost
ugly	hot	easy	entrance	confined
straight	go	clean	contract	captivity
worse	reveal	assemble/gather	success	enemy/foe
small	praise	multiply	bold	back
sweet	free	up	foul-play	

Opposites
Page 31

smile	early	few	happiness	bitter
empty	fat	seldom	danger	give
past	captivity	new	often	short
fleshy/fat	heavy/dark	transparent	unselfish	wild
mean	dead/die	shut	buy	permanent
dwarf	short	in	junior	here
come	found	future	deep	those
bad	soft/quiet	war	long	these
innocent	hate	motorist	hide	bold
easy	high	temporary	open	enormous
love	sane	ornate/fancy	plural	bottom
light	minimum	unpleasant	smart	opaque
depth	sad	singular	fast	untruth/lie
heaven	maximum	impolite/rude	large	beautiful
there	majority	rich	slovenly	separate
villain	spendthrift	wealth	rough	occupied
cowardly	happy	weak/	drunk	clear
reveal	ancient	powerless	hard	mountain/
low	evening	condemn	hollow	hill
solid	pedestrian	absent	north	defeat
abroad	valley	public	sweet	wax
dishonest	stationary	poverty	cramped	peace
cold	divide	humble	miser	wane
proud	wide	sell	fresh	strong
knowledgeable	foreign	answer	mobile	poverty
minute	far	noisy/loud	gradual	east
superior	always	slow	bow	dry
guilty	old	accept	crooked	black
separate	day	advance	weak	tame
senior	silence	advance	clever	unwise
adult	all	conceal	failure	better
sea	south	poor	winter	right
first	everywhere	wrong/left	inferior	old
		polite/courteous		age

2. *(a)* **By Adding Prefix**

disadvantage	indirect	illegible	disorder	unsafe
disapprove	inessential	dislike	impatient	insane
inaudible	unfair	unlock	imperfect	unscrew
unaware	infamous	disloyal	displeasure	unselfish
misbehave	misfire	immodest	non-poisonous	nonsense
uncomfortable	unhappy	immoral	impolite	untidy
uncommon	inhuman	immortal	impossible	intransitive
disconnect	unjust	unnecessary	improper	mistrust
discontent	unkind	ignoble	impure	untwist
inconvenient	unknown	abnormal	irregular	invisible
incorrect	illegal	disobey	irreverent	unwise

Opposites

Pages 32 – 33
    (b) By Changing Prefix
        descend, discourage, import, interior, internal, decrease, outside.

    (c) By Changing Suffix
        careless, cheerless, joyless, merciless, pitiless, useless.

Exercises in Opposites

1. failure, invisible, condemn, opaque, foul-play, depart, everywhere, fertile, modern, unwise.
2. inaudible, misbehave, unknown, illegible, immodest, ignoble, disobedient, irregular, nonsense, unpleasant.
3. south   impossible   exit   seldom   smooth
   friend/ally   motorist   sweet   innocent   junior
4. a stupid boy   a dull colour   a dim light
   a calm day   a smooth sea   a peaceful meeting
   a quiet boy   a tame horse   a cultivated flower.
5. an unarmed man   a genuine gift   a sharp answer
   I am glad   a light load   a weak/feeble/puny army
   to be out of step   to sing out of tune   she was fair
6. (1) ugly   (2) dull   (3) descent   (4) permanent   (5) sold
   (6) industrious   (7) dearth/scarcity   (8) unintelligent   (9) smooth   (10) barren
7. *(a)* answer   *(b)* re-captured   *(c)* full   *(d)* rude   *(e)* forgotten

SYNONYMS

Page 34

1. understand; vacant/unoccupied; enough; neighbourhood; tried; foes; dangerous; buy; see/understand/notice; new/up-to-date.
2. shining   strange/odd   suitable/handy   high   vanish
   join   trick   edge   bravery   anger
3. The pretty girl admired the handsome prince.
   The proud king laughed at the vain little girl.
   A stout woman should not eat fat meat.
   Weak tea will not refresh the feeble old lady.
   On a sultry day don't drink hot liquids.
   The old man was fond of antique furniture.
   Her loving hands had prepared a tender chicken.
   The day was dull and we felt quite sad.

Synonyms

Page 34

Note: There is of course no ONE correct answer to each of these questions. The following are merely examples.

4. I will <u>learn</u> to drive.
   He tried to <u>teach</u> him to swim.
   Grief disordered the old lady's mind and she became quite <u>mad</u>.
   They were <u>angry</u> when they heard they had been cheated.
   He tried to <u>invent</u> a new rocket.
   It was difficult to <u>discover</u> the whereabouts of the missing child.
   It was not <u>possible</u> to get all the books on one shelf.
   It is <u>probable</u> that they will succeed as they have tried so hard.
   She had to <u>accept</u> the offer for the house.
   They were all admitted to the hall, <u>except</u> one family.

5. *(a)* The pail <u>fell</u> into the well.
   (b) "Don't <u>hide</u> your real feelings."
   (c) I was <u>surprised</u> to find the house empty.
   (d) He <u>changes</u> his plans <u>yearly</u>.

SIMILAR WORDS

Page 36

Note: There is of course no ONE correct answer to each of these questions. The following are merely examples.

1. He shot the <u>bear</u>.
   The ground was completely <u>bare</u>.
   He acted stupidly at the party and behaved like a <u>fool</u>.
   The glass was <u>full</u> of water.
   She picked the <u>flower</u> in the garden.
   <u>Flour</u> is used to make bread.
   We were <u>too</u> late for the dance.
   The <u>two</u> dogs ran away.
   The children <u>ate</u> the cakes.
   We arrived at <u>eight</u> o'clock.
   They will <u>write</u> letters to their friends.
   He hurt his <u>right</u> hand and could not do his work.

2. She bought some <u>steak</u>.
   We have found a <u>hoard</u> of candles.
   The boy broke a <u>pane</u> of glass.
   <u>Their</u> books are on the desks.
   The wounded soldier uttered a loud <u>groan</u>.
   The joiner <u>bored</u> a small <u>hole</u> in the <u>wood</u>.
   The bicycle was for <u>sale</u>.
   The <u>whole</u> army marched into the town.
   We walked to the golf <u>course</u>.
   The girl had to <u>wait</u> till four o'clock.

Similar Words

Page 36

Note: There is no ONE correct sentence describing these occupations. The following are merely examples.

3. The man's <u>collar</u> was rather too big for his thin neck.
   The telephone <u>caller</u> rang off.
   They tried to <u>steal</u> the money.
   <u>Steel</u> is used to make cars and build ships.
   He <u>heard</u> her call.
   The <u>herd</u> of buffalo was chased by the cowboys.
   Queen Victoria's <u>reign</u> was one of the longest in history.
   It started to <u>rain</u> in the afternoon.
   <u>Their</u> pencils were new and unsharpened.
   <u>There</u> was a dog in the wood.

4. It is not <u>allowed</u> to speak <u>aloud</u> in class.
   The <u>maid</u> admitted that she had <u>made</u> a mistake.
   He will give no <u>peace</u> until he receives a <u>piece</u> of cake.
   "Did you get the <u>scent</u> I <u>sent</u> you?"
   I saw him <u>stare</u> at the man on the <u>stair</u>.
   "<u>Waste</u> not, want not", said the woman with the thin <u>waist</u>.

5. A <u>hoard</u> of coins was found under the floor.
   The business man made a large <u>profit</u> on the deal.
   He was told not to <u>meddle</u> with the toys.
   I saw the lambs <u>gambol</u> in the field.
   His name was printed in large <u>gilt</u> letters.

WORD BUILDING

Page 36

Forming Nouns:

Note: In many cases in this section more than one answer may be permissible.

ability	advertisement	attendance	boyhood	conclusion	decency
absence	amusement	attraction	bravery	contentment	decision
abundance	anger	baggage	brightness	creation	depth
accuracy	anxiety	beauty	cashier	creditor	departure
acquaintance	appearance	beggar	childhood	cruelty	description
action	applause	beginning	civilisation	curiosity	destruction
admiration	application	behaviour	cleanliness	darkness	development
adoption	approval	bitterness	comparison	deceit	discovery

Word Building

Page 37

division	grandeur	likeness	opposition	satisfaction	tale
deed	greatness	life	persuasion	scholar	thought
encouragement	growth	listener	pleasure	science	thrift
enjoyment	hatred	length	profession	security	type
equality	heroism	loss	prosperity	sight	vanity
exhaustion	height	loyalty	pride	selection	visitor
expectation	holiness	magician	proof	serenity	warrior
explanation	imagination	manliness	pursuit	shadow	warmth
faithfulness	imitation	marriage	readiness	sickness	weakness
falsehood	injury	merriment	reality	simplicity	weariness
fame	interference	missionary	rebellion	speech	weight
favour	introduction	mockery	receipt	stealth	width
food	invention	morality	recognition	streamer	wisdom
fragrance	judgement	mountaineer	revelation	striker	worthiness
freedom	justice	movement	revival	strength	youth
friendship	knowledge	musician	sadness	success	
gaiety	learning	occupation			

Page 37

Forming Adjectives:

accidental	cowardly	fortunate	mineral	quarrelsome	tidal
adventurous	crafty	French	mischievous	ragged	tiresome/tiring
affectionate	creditable	friendly	mountainous	reasonable	troublesome
angelic	criminal	gigantic	mournful	scientific	truthful/true
angry	critical	girlish	musical	sensible	valuable
anxious	cruel	golden	mysterious	shadowy	vain
athletic	customary	graceful	national	showery	various
attractive	dangerous	grevious	natural	silken	victorious
autumnal	decisive	hateful	neglectful	silvery	vocal
beautiful	descriptive	hot	noisy	sisterly	volcanic
biblical	disastrous	high	northern	skilful	Welsh
boyish	distant	heroic	noticeable	sorrowful	warlike
brazen	dutiful	hopeful/hopeless	obedient	southern	watery
breathless	energetic	iron-clad	occasional	spiral	wavy
British	expressive	Italian	ornamental	spirited	wearisome
careful	faithful	joyful	parental	starry	western
cautious	famous	lawful	patient	stopping	wintry
changeable	fashionable	lengthy	peaceful	studious	wise

Word Building

Page 37

charitable	fatherly	lifelike/living	perilous	strong	witty
childish	faulty	lovely	personal	successful	wooden
choral	favourite	luxurious	picturesque	sunny	woollen
circular	fiery	manly	pitiful/pitiless	stormy	worthy
colonial	fifth	marvellous	pleasant	sympathetic	wretched
comfortable	foolish	meddlesome	poetical	talkative	yearly
continental	forceful	melodious	poisonous	terrible/terrifying	young
courageous	forgetful	merciful/merciless	proud	thirsty	

Page 38

Forming Verbs

to	to	to	to	to	to
enable	colonise	fertilise	horrify	please	soften
act	compose	refine	enjoy	prove	solve
banish	encourage	feed	justify	provide	sing
bathe	create	enforce	kneel	purify	sparkle
beautify	criticise	befriend	know	relieve	speak
bleed	accustom	freeze	enlarge	reside	strengthen
brighten	darken	fill	live	resolve	succeed
broaden	do	glaze	lengthen	enrich	terrify
encamp	describe	glorify	magnetise	roll/enrol	think
encircle	dictate	gild	moisten	sharpen	tighten
circulate	educate	graze	nationalise	shelve	entomb
civilise	falsify	grieve	obey	shorten	try
cleanse	fatten	grow	imperil	simplify	widen
clothe					

Forming Adverbs:

ably	happily	joyfully	sweetly	thoughtfully	wearily
critically	heavily	purely	terribly	truly	widely
faithfully	horribly	simply			

COMPOUND WORDS

Sample answers in alphabetical order of first words.

blackboard	doormat	gentleman	jampot	strongroom
bootblack	dustman	gunfire	lamplight	tablecloth
churchyard	eggcup	heartache	milkmaid	timepiece
coalman	firefly	housewife	millpond	tombstone
daylight	football	inkpot	schoolmaster	toothpick

Word Building

Page 38

Note: In many cases in this section more than one answer may be permissible.

1. pleasure, proof, knowledge, pride, choice, encouragement, strength, reality, justice, gift.
2. gaiety; selection; growth; baggage; action, actor; receipt, receiver; invitation; success, succession; repentance; division.
3. British; hot; expensive; angry; faithful, faithless; high; fashionable; boyish; vain; sensible, senseless.

Page 39

4.
decide	decisive	mystery	mysterious
bible	biblical	voice	vocal
talk	talkative	nation	national
circle	circular	winter	wintry
attract	attractive	peril	perilous

5.
knee	to kneel	tight	to tighten
strong	to strengthen	grief	to grieve
description	to describe	large	to enlarge
gold	to gild	glory	to glorify
custom	to accustom	food	to feed

6.
obedient	to obey	sweet	to sweeten
education	to educate	fat	to fatten
life	to live	composition	to compose
civil	to civilise	tomb	to entomb
bath	to bathe	pure	to purify

7.
Adjective	Noun	Verb
long	length	to lengthen
strong	strength	to strengthen
broad	breadth	to broaden
glad	gladness	to gladden
able	ability	to enable
wide	width	to widen

CORRECT USAGE

THE VERB

Page 42

1. arose, broke, cut, fell, kept
   said, shook, drank, bit, chose
2. borne, driven, flown, given, hurt
   ridden, sold, spoken, come, swum
3. eat, beat, freeze, hide, blow, speak, awake, sell, lose.
4. to burn, to speak, to stand, to sweep, to drive.

The Verb

Page 43

5. | Past Tense | Past Participle | Past Tense | Past Participle |
|---|---|---|---|
| was | been | did | done |
| forgot | forgotten | grew | grown |
| wrote | written | sang | sung |
| tore | torn | hid | hidden |
| went | gone | began | begun |

6. | Present Tense | Past Tense | Past Participle |
|---|---|---|
| I rise | I rose | I have risen |
| I forget | I forgot | I have forgotten |
| I cut | I cut | I have cut |
| I sing | I sang | I have sung |
| I blow | I blew | I have blown |

7. (a) When he met the lady he raised his hat.
    (b) Yesterday the boy rose at five o'clock.
    (c) I saw him rise from his seat.
    (d) She tried to raise the lid.
    (e) The sun had risen in the sky.

8. She had gone for a walk.　　　　　He saw his uncle yesterday.
    The old man fell asleep in his chair.
    He was awakened by the noise.　　The boy was dreaming about pirates.

Which word is correct?

1. We drank our tea before we sang the carol.
2. After he had run about five kilometres, he sank to the ground.
3. Cloth is woven from wool which has grown on sheep.
4. He had given me the parcel before he was taken a prisoner.
5. The timid creature was driven into a narrow valley where it was soon slain by the cruel tiger.
6. The vessel sank before they had swum a great distance.
7. The tree had fallen across the road and many of its branches were broken.
8. By the time the sun had risen the aeroplane had flown across the sea.
9. No sooner had he spoken than a deer sprang into our path.
10. He began to look for the toy which he had given to his brother.
11. The man had thrown away the purse which was stolen from the lady.
12. I have known him since he has come to this village.

Page 44

13. The jacket had been well worn and the cloth had shrunk.
14. After we had eaten our supper we went to the pond which was frozen over.
15. The picture was drawn by a famous and wealthy artist who had risen from poverty.
16. They had just gone when we were seen by our friends.
17. A nest had fallen to the ground, where it had been blown by the wind.
18. The bell rang just after I had written the letter.

Correct Usage

Page 45

Some Common Verbs with Suitable Adverbs

1. He charged furiously.   He decided immediately.   He slept soundly.
   He crept silently.   He spent sparingly.   He fell heavily.
   He smiled broadly.   He waited patiently.

2. The girl sings sweetly.   The clerk wrote carefully.
   The lion roars loudly.   The river flows gently.
   The artist paints beautifully.   The stars shine brightly.
   The child sleeps soundly.   The horse gallops proudly.
   The cat walks stealthily.   The man frowns angrily.

Comparison of Adjectives

Page 46

1. | Positive | Comparative | Superlative |
   | --- | --- | --- |
   | many | more | most |
   | hot | hotter | hottest |
   | bad | worse | worst |
   | famous | more famous | most famous |
   | little | less | least |

2. **Comparatives**
   faster   better   more gracious
   taller   more beautiful

3. **Superlatives**
   thinnest   most   most comfortable
   gayest   most handsome

4. | Positive | Comparative | Superlative |
   | --- | --- | --- |
   | long | longer | longest |
   | far | farther | farthest |
   | good | better | best |
   | generous | more generous | most generous |
   | late | later | latest |
   | cautious | more cautious | most cautious |

5. nearest .... superlative   better .... comparative
   far .... positive   more certain .... comparative
   surest .... superlative   larger .... comparative
   most wonderful .... superlative   bad .... positive
   shorter .... comparative   biggest .... superlative

CONCORD

Page 48

Each of the boys <u>is</u> going on holiday so each of them <u>has</u> gone to bed early.
Everybody <u>was</u> pleased as each of them <u>was</u> treated alike.
Neither he nor she <u>wants</u> to go.
Weren't we sorry when we heard you <u>were</u> going?
All but Tom <u>have</u> been lazy, so all but Tom <u>lose</u> marks.
James, as well as John, <u>rises</u> at eight, so James, like John, <u>is</u> early for work.
Neither of the singers <u>was</u> present.
The miller and his wife <u>are</u> a happy couple.
Neither of them <u>has</u> paid as both of them <u>are</u> poor.
The girl, with several others, <u>was</u> going to school.
Both Agnes and Albert <u>are</u> here tonight.
John, like James, <u>is</u> smaller than Peter.
All of you but Andrew <u>are</u> good, so all of you but Andrew <u>get</u> a reward.
Each of the ladies <u>is</u> delighted as each of the ladies <u>receives</u> a prize.
Anybody <u>is</u> allowed to enter.
Nobody <u>is</u> grumpy at the camp because nobody <u>is</u> allowed to feel lonely.
Arthur as well as Donald <u>is</u> clever so Arthur as well as Donald has succeeded.
The gentlemen and the ladies <u>were</u> wearing evening dress.
Either one or the other <u>is</u> wealthy, as either one or the other <u>has</u> plenty of money.
All of us but David <u>were</u> on holiday so all of us but David <u>are</u> suntanned.
<u>Weren't</u> they pleased when they heard we <u>were</u> coming?
Cecil as well as Annie <u>likes</u> spelling and Cecil as well as Annie hates arithmetic.
Why <u>does</u> every one of them do that, when every one of them knows the arrangements?
Neither the officer nor the soldiers <u>were</u> afraid. (See page 47 *(i)* — Rules of Concord.)
Either you <u>have</u> to take the blame or your brother <u>has</u> to.

THE PRONOUN

Page 51

<u>He</u> and <u>I</u> went for a walk.
It was <u>he</u> <u>whom</u> we saw in the shop.
No one believes it was <u>she</u>; everyone thinks it was <u>I</u>.
Between <u>him</u> and <u>me</u> we ate the whole cake.
<u>She</u> and <u>I</u> can go, but <u>you</u> and <u>he</u> cannot.
Jack is not as clever as <u>he</u> or <u>I</u>.
It seems to be <u>they</u>.
Between you and <u>me</u>, be careful what you say to Annie or her.
<u>She</u> and <u>you</u> sang very well together.
Let you and <u>me</u> go to the shore.

23

The Pronoun

Page 51

John is much brighter than he.
Those are they.
This discovery must remain a secret between you and me.
Jean and she ran to the house.
It was he who knew the right answer.
James is older than I, but his brothers are younger than we.
The dog pursued Frank and me.
Who are they?
We were busy when he and his brother appeared.
Let him and me fetch the small table.
We lads were at the cinema.
Between you and me, I know all about Sue and her.
He is almost as big as I.
Her sisters are smaller than we, but she is taller than I.
You and he, if you played together, would become friends.
The wild creature snarled at my sister and me.
They will choose either him or her.
You and I if we try, would manage it, but you and he couldn't.
It appears to be he.
She and I are twelve years of age.
Her cousin is younger than she.
Was it I you saw there?
Who did it? I did it.
I spoke to him and her.
I saw the book but it was they who tore it.
The dress becomes her better than me.
We are certain it was not he.
It is not she that I am angry with.
Him I can excuse but not them.
Was it he or she who found the purse?
Whom do you think we met?
Is that he at the door? (more correct),
but
Is that him at the door? (would be universally accepted).

THE CONJUNCTION

Pages 54 – 55

TIME

(1) Wait there <u>till</u> I have finished.
(2) He left <u>before</u> darkness fell.
(3) We have remained here <u>since</u> you left.
(4) <u>After</u> they arrived, they sat down.
(5) I can call <u>whenever</u> it is convenient to you.
(6) The exercise will be corrected <u>when</u> it is finished.
(7) His brother waited <u>until</u> James returned.
(8) She read a book <u>while</u> I wrote a letter.

PLACE

(1) The place <u>whence</u> the stranger came was not on the map.
(2) The faithful dog followed his master <u>wherever</u> he went.
(3) The old man pointed out the place <u>where</u> he lived.
(4) We will go <u>whither</u> our fancy takes us.

CAUSE OR REASON

(1) <u>As</u> we left early, we did not see him.
(2) I was afraid to speak <u>lest</u> he should tell.
(3) You ask him, <u>since</u> you are friends.
(4) My uncle was angry <u>because</u> he was deceived.

CONCESSION

(1) The boy is strong and healthy <u>though</u> he is not tall.
(2) <u>While</u> I trust him, I dislike his companions.
(3) We will go <u>even if</u> it rains.
(4) <u>Whether</u> you like it or not, he will invite you.
(5) My cold is much worse <u>although</u> I have tried to cure it.

CONDITION

(1) He could not win <u>unless</u> he was given a start.
(2) I'll lend you an umbrella <u>if</u> it rains.
(3) She will go <u>if</u> you ask her.
(4) You cannot obtain admission <u>unless</u> you pay.

MANNER or DEGREE

(1) You are quite right <u>as far as</u> I can see.
(2) The dog lifted his paw <u>as though</u> he understood me.
(3) She is older <u>than</u> I am.
(4) They did not play <u>so well as</u> their opponents.
(5) The man looked <u>as if</u> he was a foreigner.
(6) I cannot work <u>as</u> he can.

The Conjunction

Page 55

PURPOSE

(1) The man put on the light <u>so that</u> he could read.
(2) <u>In order that</u> they might be in time, they left early.
(3) The boy ran quickly <u>lest</u> he should be left behind.
(4) You should go <u>that</u> you may be cured.

CONSEQUENCE

(1) It was so misty <u>that</u> the search was called off.
(2) The dog ran so fast <u>that</u> he caught the hare.

THE PREPOSITION

Pages 55 – 56

1.   (1) The boy must apologise <u>to</u> the lady.
   (2) That man is an authority <u>on</u> flowers.
   (3) The mother was proud <u>of</u> her son's success.
   (4) He placed the bat <u>against</u> the wall.
   (5) My cousin put the book <u>in</u> the drawer.
   (6) It is an exception <u>to</u> the rule.
   (7) His opinion differs <u>from</u> mine.
   (8) The man ran <u>down/along/up</u> the path.
   (9) She takes great pride <u>in</u> her appearance.
   (10) The ball went <u>through/towards</u> the window.

2.   (1) The pencil lay on/under/beside/near/underneath/below/behind the desk.
   (2) The man rowed across/on/over/up/down the river.
   (3) The lady sat beside/near/behind/beyond/by/with the chairman.

3.   (1) I stood <u>on</u> the bridge <u>of</u> the ship.
   (2) <u>Above</u> me, I saw a cloudy sky.
   (3) The dog leaped <u>over</u> the wall <u>after</u> a ball.
   (4) We chased him <u>through</u> a field <u>of</u> hay.
   (5) <u>With</u> that ticket you can obtain admission <u>to</u> the show.
   (6) My brother received a letter <u>from</u> him.
   (7) The farmer stored his hay <u>in</u> a large barn.
   (8) <u>Beside</u> the boxes lay several boulders.
   (9) The careless boy ran <u>behind</u> the car.
   (10) <u>During</u> the year many people were injured <u>in</u> street accidents.

CORRECTION OF SENTENCES

Pages 57 – 58

1. She was the older of the two sisters.
2. Whom did you see at the party?
3. Neither John nor James was present.
4. She is not as old as I.
5. The better team won the football match.
6. The books that we read were interesting.
7. As it was a fine day I went to the seashore.
8. For whom can it be?
9. He was angry with me for leaving.
10. I am, yours truly.
11. I cannot run any further.
12. John has broken his leg.
13. "Hurrah!" shouted the man.
14. The letter was sent to Mr. John Brown OR John Brown Esq..
15. The parcel was returned to the sender.
16. I left home at a quarter to seven.
17. The girl said that she did it herself.
18. He returned home as quickly as he could.
19. I have forgotten to post the letter.
20. "Where are my boots?"
21. She hurt her leg.
22. She had a bad accident.
23. There are four books on the table.
24. He went to get up.
25. The lady bought a comb with plastic teeth for the baby.
26. Between you and me, he is quite wrong.
27. They sang the same song twice.
28. This jacket is worn out.
29. It's no use my working.
30. I intended to write.
31. I was so tired I could hardly have spoken.
32. The fishermen saw a shoal of herring in the sea.
33. Everyone in the class knows he or she could do better.
34. Between you and me we saw many people.
35. I saw a dog, which had a long tail, with his master.
36. We found the ring made of gold, belonging to the lady.
    OR
    We found the gold ring belonging to the lady.
37. A piano with carved legs was sold to a lady.
38. We saw the rascal who stole our ball.
39. There are five books on the table.
40. A man and his dog were at the corner.
41. She and her husband are going.

Correction of Sentences

Page 58

42. His hair badly needs cutting.
43. Neither of them is tall.
44. Someone has left his or her books behind.
45. He and his sister went to the pictures.
46. My friend and I went to buy coats for ourselves.
47. It was he whom you saw.
48. They have done it again.
49. She could not come any quicker.
50. We have never seen any of them.
51. He couldn't remember anything.
52. He did his work correctly.
53. Is he the taller of the two?
54. Each of the boys had his books.
55. It was I that broke the window.
56. Who is the cleverer, John or Mary?
57. A kinder man never lived.
58. I was so breathless I could hardly speak.
59. The animal did not take any notice.
60. Neither of them has been lucky.
61. He and I went to the pictures together.
62. He took the bigger portion.
    OR
    He took half.
63. It was a remarkably fine picture.
64. He is worse than I.
65. I saw him go to the theatre.
66. One of the horses was tired.
67. Of the two, I like James better.
68. Give me those oranges.
69. He doesn't speak very clearly.
70. We are quite sure he did it.
71. She sent it to you and me.
72. The man taught him to swim.
73. That answer is different from mine.
74. Neither one nor the other is right.
75. I do not think she will stay.
76. The lady sings quite nicely.
77. He did not accept the gift.
78. To whom does this belong?
79. Who do you think that can be?
80. The two brothers divided the apple between them.

THE RIGHT WORD IN THE RIGHT PLACE

Pages 59 – 60

1. (1) His watch stopped at six o'clock.
   (2) I remember how the story ended.
   (3) I have completed my lessons. (Could use "finished".)
   (4) They have finished the alterations. (Could use "completed".)
   (5) The meeting concluded with the National Anthem.
   (6) Having enough money they closed the fund.

2. a beautiful garden   a pretty bonnet   a delicious cake
   a pleasant/good walk   a fine house   an agreeable man
   a good/pleasant day   a convenient train   an enjoyable concert
   an interesting book.

3. He sang tunefully.   He chuckled gleefully.
   He frowned angrily.   He smiled broadly.
   He bowed humbly.   He listened attentively.
   He mumbled indistinctly.   He whispered softly.

4. He said that he would come.   He shouted with joy.
   He explained why he was late.   "Look!" he exclaimed.
   He pleaded for mercy.   He muttered under his breath.
   He whispered quietly to his neighbour.   "That is so," he answered.

5. He charged furiously.   He ate greedily.
   He bled profusely.   He slept soundly.
   He pulled vigorously.   He strove manfully.
   He caressed fondly.   He crept stealthily.

6. He rose at eight o'clock.
   He received a penny from his mother.
   He ate (had, took) his breakfast early.
   He caught a bad cold yesterday.
   He arrived at the station in time.
   He was married last year.

7. A man who digs for coal is a <u>miner</u>.
   I switched on the <u>electric</u> light.
   The <u>Christmas</u> holiday is in December.
   They sang a Christmas <u>carol</u>.
   He was so ill <u>that</u> he went to bed.
   The postman <u>delivered</u> the letters.
   He avoided accidents because he drove very <u>carefully</u>.

8. (1) That is the boy <u>who</u> broke the window.
   (2) That is the stone <u>which</u> broke the window.
   (3) That is the man <u>whose</u> window was broken.
   (4) That is the boy <u>whom</u> I saw breaking the window.
   (5) That is the boy <u>who</u> told me that he broke the window.

The Right Word in the Right Place

9. (1) table   (2) stable   (3) fable   (4) portable
   (5) valuable   (6) cable   (7) unable   (8) arable
   (9) vegetable   (10) breakable

10. (1) depart   (2) return   (3) descend   (4) advance
    (5) enter   (6) crawl   (7) leave   (8) hurry
    (9) amble   (10) ascend

11. (1) Plunge it into cold water.
    (2) Ask someone — preferably a policeman if available.
    (3) Sit down, rub the ankle, and as soon as possible wrap it round tightly with a bandage.
    (4) Sit down, and tilt your head slightly forward.
    (5) Open the windows — and find an adult to turn off the gas and phone the Gas Company
    (6) Roll her on the ground in a coat or rug.
    (7) Take it to the nearest police station.
    (8) Run cold water on it, dry it gently and bandage it.
    (9) Telephone the Fire Brigade — and the police if necessary.
    (10) Remove the sting, and treat it with ointment.

ADDITION OF CLAUSES

Page 61

Sample answers

		Kind of clause
1.	I saw the lady ... who lives next door.	adjectival
2.	The little boy said ... that he was lost.	noun
3.	The girl ran quickly ... because she was late.	adverbial (reason)
4.	They opened the door ... when they reached home.	principal
5.	I noticed ... that the audience quietened down ... when he rose to speak.	noun
6.	We stood on the very spot ... where he died.	adjectival
7.	Do not go into the water ... if you cannot swim.	principal
8.	The dog barked loudly ... when he saw the postman.	adverbial (time)
9.	The lady ... who was run over ... was my sister.	adjectival
10.	"Will you let me know ... as soon as it arrives?"	adverbial (time)
11.	The dog ... plunged into the water and ... saved the child.	principal
12.	We saw the train ... as it entered the tunnel.	adverbial (time)
13.	I hope ... they will understand.	noun
14.	He stood up ... while they listened.	principal
15.	The boy hurt himself badly ... when he fell down.	adverbial (time)
16.	The man ... who broke into the house ... was caught by the police.	adjectival

Addition of Clauses

Page 61

		Kind of clause
17.	I saw ... <u>what was going on</u>.	noun
18.	She bought an umbrella ... <u>because it was raining</u>.	adverbial (reason)
19.	<u>She trembled</u> ... as she spoke.	principal
20.	The messenger arrived ... <u>when it stopped raining</u>.	adverbial (time)
21.	I watched the man ... <u>who was cutting his hedge</u>.	adjectival
22.	I do not know ... <u>how long it takes</u>.	noun
23.	As the girl approached the house ... <u>she started to shout</u>.	principal
24.	We saw ... <u>no-one was at home</u> ... when we returned.	noun
25.	<u>Call the doctor</u> ... if you are ill.	principal
26.	"Come to my house ... <u>when you have completed the work</u>."	adverbial (time)
27.	I know the child ... <u>who ran away from school</u>.	adjectival
28.	When I came here ... <u>the place was just farmland</u>.	principal
29.	I bought a stamp ... which cost very little.	principal
30.	My father scolded me ... <u>because I had lost the ball</u>.	adverbial (reason)
31.	The crowd rushed forward ... <u>when they saw the queen</u>.	adverbial (time)
32.	The soldiers, <u>who had followed the enemy</u> ... were trapped in the wood.	adjectival
33.	The unhappy scholar said ... <u>he was tired of his work</u>.	noun
34.	<u>I will probably forget all about it</u> ... if you do not send word.	principal
35.	The boy lifted the box ... <u>which was blocking the way</u>.	adjectival
36.	The man waved frantically ... <u>and managed to attract attention</u>.	principal

PHRASES TO CLAUSES

Page 62

1. He failed ... <u>because he was careless</u>.
2. <u>When his task was completed</u> ... the boy went out to play.
3. He told me ... <u>that he was coming</u>.
4. A man ... <u>who holds a high position</u> ... has many responsibilities.
5. She lived in a cottage ... <u>which was near the sea</u>.
6. <u>When I entered</u> ... I saw several pictures.
7. The police recovered the property ... <u>which had been stolen</u>.
8. We do not know ... <u>where he is hiding</u>.

Clauses into Phrases

1. I am convinced ... <u>of his sincerity</u>.
2. The child was in bed ... <u>before sunset</u>.
3. His action showed ... <u>his bravery</u>.
4. I am certain ... <u>of your help</u>.
5. <u>On approaching</u> ... I heard a great noise.

SENTENCES

Pages 62 – 63

Simple to Complex

1. I have a dog of which I am very fond.
2. That is the man who stole my purse.
3. I was travelling in a bus which collided with a taxi.
4. The boy did not pass because his work was badly done.
5. I was gazing out of the window when I saw a crowd.
6. The boy was riding a horse which looked tired.
7. The man could hardly walk because he carried such a heavy load.
8. The book, which is red, belongs to Jack.
9. The girl went for the doctor, who stayed next door.
10. The house, which was built by Tom's father, was destroyed.
11. He works hard at his lessons because he wishes to succeed.
12. The men, who were walking quickly, saw me.
13. He heard the strains of music as he was passing a church.
14. The lady lost the book while she was going to the library.
15. The man stood at the door, which was open.
16. The boy took home the rabbit which he had caught.
17. The girl hurt herself when she fell heavily.
18. He saw many books when he opened the cupboard.
19. The lady who lost her purse, was careless.
20. Mary entered the room which was brightly decorated.
21. When a loud peal of thunder came the children were frightened..
22. Tom made mistakes in reading because he could not see well.
23. The teacher praised the boys because they had worked well.
24. The horse fell as it was pulling a heavy load.
25. The man, who caught a salmon, took it home.
26. The boy cannot walk because he has hurt his foot.
27. The lady sat in a coach which was drawn by four horses.
28. The tourist climbed the hill, which was steep.
29. Because she has a good voice, my sister sings in the choir.
30. The girl found a brooch which she took to her mother.
31. I found a lady's purse which contained two coins.
32. The girl who wore a red dress, sat next to me.
33. I visited the little cottage in which I was born.
34. The woman who stood at the corner of the street, was selling flowers.
35. I went to see my cousin whose home was in the country.
36. I gave money to the man, who was poorly clad.

Complex to Simple

1. He is a man. He is very intelligent.
2. We heard the news. He was saved.
3. How old is he? I can tell you.
4. The woman lives in a house. It is very big.
5. He spoke to the soldier. The soldier was wounded.
6. The boy lost his ticket. He was careless.
7. He will arrive. Then I shall speak to him.
8. The child found a ring. It was very valuable.

ALPHABETICAL ORDER

Page 64

1. colonel; extremely; humorous; judgment; language; necessary; official; vegetable.
2. pail; pain; pale; pane; pore; pour; pray; prey.

THE APOSTROPHE

Page 64

1. (1) The boy's pencil lay on the floor.
   (2) The ladies' coats were in the cloakroom.
   (3) My cousin's hand was badly hurt.
   (4) The men's boots were covered with mud.
   (5) The child's doll fell into the pond.

2. (1) The children's books were left in my uncle's house.
   (2) The maid's dress was torn by a neighbour's dog.
   (3) My father's wallet was discovered in the thieves' den.
   (4) A duck's egg is generally cheaper than a hen's.
   (5) Mr. Smith's watch is five minutes slower than Mr. Brown's.

PUNCTUATION

Page 66

1. "What time is it?" asked the traveller.
2. His father said, "Where is your brother's knife?"
3. My friends exclaimed, "What a lovely view!"
4. "He has gone to school," said his sister, in a quiet voice.
5. The child suddenly shouted, "Look!"
6. "Oh!" cried the boy. "I have hurt my finger."
7. "Come here," said his mother. "All right," replied the boy.
8. The man asked, "Have you seen the hammer?"
   "Yes," replied his companion. "It is on the table."
9. A boy said to his chum, "Are you going to the pictures?"
   "No," replied the other. "I'm on my way home."
10. "When I return," said the girl to her father, "will you tell me the story of the shipwreck?"
    "Very well," he answered, "but don't be too long at your aunt's."

POPULAR PHRASES

Page 73

horse play	rough, boisterous play.
from pillar to post	(driven) from one problem to another.
as the crow flies	in a straight line; the shortest way.
no flies on him	not easily deceived.
a red letter day	a special, memorable day of great joy or success.
a dead cert	an absolute certainty.
a far cry	something very different (from the matter in hand).

Popular Phrases
Page 73

a fly in the ointment	trouble in a situation.
on the nail	(payment for something) immediately on demand.
bats in the belfry	eccentricity, near madness.
back to the wall	in a dangerous situation from which there is no retreat and where one must defend oneself.
a fine kettle of fish	a mess, muddle, awkward state of affairs.
a busman's holiday	using spare time to do something which you usually do anyway.
a white elephant	a possession, creation or achievement ultimately proved useless.
not worth the candle	something which is unrewarding, considering the effort involved.
a cat on hot bricks	an excited, worried person, unable to concentrate.
with flying colours	achieving something with triumphant success.
every man Jack	everybody.
not a patch on	totally inferior to — not to be compared with.
a storm in a teacup	trouble over nothing; out of proportion to the matter concerned.
for a lark	for a prank, a joke.
a bird's eye view	an overall picture — seeing everything complete, as from above.
a stiff upper lip	self-control in a difficult situation.
a blind alley	an undertaking which gives no chance of ultimate success.
a hen on a hot girdle	a person acting distractedly and unmethodically.
a cock and bull story	a totally improbable, invented explanation.
a flash in the pan	a single, instant success, never again achieved.
the lion's share	the major portion.
pins and needles	a tingling sensation in a limb which has been cramped and to which the blood is re-circulating.
by hook or by crook	by any means, fair or foul.

GENERAL KNOWLEDGE
Pages 76 – 78

1. bully
2. crew, sailors
3. shepherd
4. submarine
5. garage
6. leaflet
7. orchard
8. clock, watch
9. milk
10. joiner, carpenter
11. oasis
12. tributary
13. century
14. compass
15. rungs
16. dalmatian (dog), leopard, cheetah
17. surgeon
18. bow, stem, prow
19. dawn
20. artist
21. ford
22. bat, owl, cat
23. fracture
24. mutton
25. barrel, can, drum
26. cemetery
27. violin, 'cello, viola, guitar
28. equator
29. thermometer
30. milk
31. sight, smell, hearing, touch, taste
32. zebra, tiger
33. aviary
34. atmosphere
35. miser
36. through its gills

General Knowledge

37. red, orange, yellow, green, blue, indigo, violet
38. attic
39. kilt
40. triangle
41. the oceans of the world
42. cabin
43. sergeant
44. six
45. foundry
46. whale, dolphin, otter
47. steam
48. pork, ham, bacon
49. tannery
50. ass
51. dynamo
52. a sailor
53. a three-legged stand
54. venison
55. contraband
56. a space traveller
57. red, blue, yellow
58. a band of stars stretching across the sky
59. a look-out position on the mast of a ship
60. leg before wicket
61. a bicycle or vehicle which jolts the passenger
62. aluminium
63. The Great Wall of China
64. aquarium
65. one who imitates another person's actions
66. backbone
67. a heavenly body that revolves round the sun
68. a picturesque cave
69. horn, trumpet, bugle, clarinet, bassoon, flute
70. restaurant
71. a group of nests where rooks live
72. all the land drained by a river and the streams that flow into it
73. the punishment by death for a crime
74. right hand side
75. sailing across the equator
76. the coat of a sheep sheared in one piece
77. drum, tambourine, xylophone triangle
78. duet
79. one aged 100 years or more
80. compasses
81. bee
82. porcupine, hedgehog
83. in an emergency — specially at sea
84. 25th December
85. thirty-two
86. ice
87. kangaroo, opossum
88. metal plate used to join rails on railway tracks
89. microscope
90. December
91. a level or tier of a multi-level building
92. lion
93. aviator
94. a hooded cloak worn by Arabs
95. bunk
96. a dandy — too well dressed
97. an umbrella
98. camel
99. Chinese two-wheeled carriage drawn by a man on foot or on a cycle
100. oxygen
101. a piece of equipment in space to send photographs of clouds back to earth
102. mosquito
103. yolk
104. Roman god of war
105. when he is short-sighted
106. chart
107. peel
108. bung
109. cure
110. cavalry
111. a wide view from above
112. an Arab chief
113. boiling water and tea leaves
114. from tin and copper
115. scholar, student, apprentice
116. magnetically formed streamers of light seen in the north of the northern hemisphere
117. husky
118. mortar
119. exit

35

General Knowledge

120. summit
121. rock-like remains of the bodies of tiny animals (found in the sea)
122. a female spirit who shrieks just before a death in the family — in Ireland or Scotland specially
123. infantry
124. quarry
125. albumen
126. wages, pay (very often monthly)
127. walking side by side
128. a plant producing coffee beans
129. a wheel with teeth round it
130. cow or other type of cattle, sheep or deer
131. a waterfall — or an eye disease
132. A, E, I, O, U, sometimes Y
133. lion, tiger, stoat, weasel
134. equipment sent to survey the moon
135. a floating device to help save someone from drowning
136. oak
137. fox
138. a long narrow boat propelled by one oarsman, used on the canals of Venice
139. apples
140. a flesh-eating creature
141. three brass balls hanging outside pawn shops, where one can borrow money by leaving possessions as security (known as 'pawning')
142. banister
143. Africa
144. America
145. giraffe
146. the meat of a calf
147. a horrific dream

GENERAL TESTS

Pages 87 – 96

TEST 1

1. She told her father — Main clause
   When the girl returned from London — Subordinate adverb clause of time
   That she had seen a grizzly bear — Subordinate noun clause
   Which performed tricks in the circus — Subordinate adjective clause

2. London — proper noun — objective case after preposition "from"
   her — possessive adjective, describing "father"
   that — conjunction
   grizzly — adjective — describing "bear"
   performed — verb (past tense)

3. (a) instructress, spinster, mare, maidservant, wife.
   (b) knives, children, pennies or pence, sheep, pianos.

4. The donkey brays. The owl hoots.
   The pig grunts. The monkey chatters.
   The frog croaks. The lamb bleats.
   The dog barks. The horse neighs.
   The wolf howls. The elephant trumpets.

5. (1) He said that you did it.
   (2) She is the bigger of the twins.
   (3) It was I that took the pencil.
   (4) The man went to get the book.
   (5) A piano, with carved legs, was sold to the lady.

General Tests

TEST 2

1. *(a)* where Burns was born — subordinate adjective clause describing "cottage"
   (b) where he was going — subordinate noun clause, object of "told"
   (c) where they found a resting place — adverb clause of place.

2. near — preposition; me — pronoun; secretly — adverb; soldiers — noun; resting — adjective

3. As black as coal (or ink).   As fast as a hare (or deer).
   As meek as a lamb   As happy as a sandboy
   As brave as a lion   As keen as mustard
   As sweet as honey   As steady as a rock
   As cold as ice (or charity)   As fit as a fiddle

4. *(a)* I — me; he — him; you — you; we — us; they — them.
   (b) does — did; hides — hid; writes — wrote; sings — sang; bites — bit.

5. (1) The child was in bed <u>before sunset</u>.
   (2) Flowers will grow <u>in suitable conditions</u>.
   (3) Remember to write <u>on arrival</u>.
   (4) I saw her <u>at 4 o'clock</u>.
   (5) I am convinced <u>of his sincerity</u>.

TEST 3

1. He discovered — Main clause
   When the gentleman arrived at his home — Adverbial clause of time
   that he had left his umbrella in the train — Subordinate noun clause

2. when — conjunction; discovered — verb (past tense); his — possessive adjective; train — noun.

3. | many | more | most | hot | hotter | hottest |
   |------|------|------|-----|--------|---------|
   | evil | more evil | most evil | famous | more famous | most famous |
   | little | less | least | | | |

4. *(a)* tent, form, caravan, eyrie, hive.
   (b) impossible, insecure, unwelcome, misuse, illegal.

5. (1) The rabbits ran from the dogs.
   (2) The girls wore blue dresses.
   (3) The sailors swam to their ships.
   (4) They had sharp knives.
   (5) We kept our birds in cages.

General Tests

TEST 4

1. *(a)* When I heard
   (b) I — personal pronoun;
   seriously — adverb;
   resolved — verb;
   possible — adjective.
   (c) infinitive. *(d)* singular.
   (e) man. *(f)* in.

2. (1) introduction, loyalty, revival, readiness, breadth.
   (2) parental, reasonable, fortunate, poetic, wintry or wintery.

3. Birds build nests by instinct.
   He was an obstinate man, and refused all advice.
   The music was very traditional, having been passed from musician to musician over many years.
   I gave £10 and £1 respectively to John and James.
   The accident was a strange occurrence, and no one could explain it.
   The metric system was standard in France before being adopted in Britain.
   She was a very respectable person, admired by many people.
   The problem will be resolved if every one thinks hard about it.

4. (1) The boy was told not to meddle <u>with</u> the pencils.
   (2) She felt ashamed <u>of</u> herself.
   (3) The man took great pride <u>in</u> his garden.
   (4) The child has been lost <u>since</u> Thursday.
   (5) He hurried home <u>from</u> school.

5. *(a)* he is poor *(f)* he is dead.
   (b) he is rather deaf *(g)* he is very brave
   (c) he is snobbish and class-conscious *(h)* taken advantage of and badly treated
   (d) he is very tired *(i)* he is an old sailor
   (e) he is listening very intently *(j)* he is not feeling well.

TEST 5

1. We were thoroughly alarmed — Main clause
   when information reached us — Subordinate adverb clause (time)
   that the train had been involved in a serious accident — Subordinate noun clause
   in which our friends were travelling — Adjective clause describing "train".

2. we — personal pronoun; thoroughly — adverb; train — noun; which — relative pronoun; serious — adjective.

3. *(a)* Al or Bert, Chris or Chrissie, Fred, Pat, Liz or Betty.
   (b) Holland, India, Greenland or Canada, Greece, Wales.

General Tests

4. "Do you think" said my friend, in a whisper, "that there's a chance of escape?" "Certainly," I replied.

5. *(a)* The ship reached harbour safe and sound.
   (b) The man was an out and out rascal.
   (c) She is head and shoulders taller than her brother.
   (d) Later through foolishness he went to rack and ruin.
   (e) The soldiers would follow their general through thick and thin.

TEST 6

1. *(a)* garden — adjective;   that — conjunction;   which — relative pronoun; was — verb;   ruins — noun.
   (b) he noticed — principal clause
   (c) in which he was born — subordinate adjective clause.
   (d) complex sentence.

2. curtains; ruler; envelope; anchor; spoon.

3. directory; atlas or map; dictionary; calendar; diary, daily newspaper.

4. broke, broken;   flew, flown;   hid, hidden;   rang, rung;   swam, swum

5. *(a)* Leave well alone and don't interfere.
   (b) Too much help or advice can be a disadvantage.
   (c) Not risking a second attempt at something when the first was a failure.

TEST 7

1. *(a)* We ran for shelter ... <u>when it started to rain</u>. — Adverbial clause of time.
   (b) When the rain stopped ... <u>we returned home</u>. — Main clause.
   (c) Mary told him ... <u>that she did not wish to see him again</u>. — Noun clause.
   (d) The cunning fox, ... <u>which escaped through the woods</u>, could not be caught. — Adjectival clause.

2. *(a)* Walk as quickly as possible.   *(b)* He has forgotten the address.
   (c) Neither Tom nor I can swim.   *(d)* This end of the rope is the thicker.
   (e) The time was a quarter past nine.

3. strong — strength; courage — encourage; obey — obedient; poverty — wealth; mute — dumb.

4. The teacher told the little boy not to <u>meddle</u> with the <u>board</u> as it had a <u>loose</u> hinge. The child went over to the <u>waste</u> paper box <u>hoping</u> to find his pencil.

5. We had cousins who stayed on those little farms. They knew that we liked to come here on our holidays.

TEST 8

1. *(a)* town — subjective (or nominative) subject of "had been deserted";
   which — objective (or accusative) object of "had ruined";
   walls — objective (or accusative); object of the verb "reached".
   (b) city — adjective;   that — conjunction;   reached — verb (past tense);
   enemy — noun; for — preposition;   some — adjective.
   (c) When the soldiers reached the city.

General Tests

2. (1) often, invisible, blame/condemn, import, retreat.
   (2) foe, buy, weak, see, hide.
3. *(a)* conductor; *(b)* steam; *(c)* barrel/drum/can; *(d)* aviary; *(e)* ambulance.
4. headache, blackboard, gentleman, dustbin, eggcup.
5. *(a)* (1) A stitch in time saves nine.
       (2) A bird in the hand is worth two in the bush.
       (3) Birds of a feather flock together.
       (4) A rolling stone gathers no moss.
       (5) First come, first served.
   (b) a.m.   *ante meridiem*, morning
       Co.   Company or County
       B.B.C.   British Broadcasting Corporation
       G.P.O.   General Post Office
       p.m.   *post meridiem*, afternoon
       M.P.   Member of Parliament or Military Police
       U.K.   United Kingdom
       A.D.   *Anno Domini* in the — year since the birth of our Lord.
       U.S.A.   United States of America
       J.P.   Justice of the Peace.

TEST 9

1. *(a)* The boys ran away <u>when the policeman appeared</u>. — Adverbial clause (time).
   (b) The lady <u>who was killed</u> was my sister. — Adjectival clause.
   (c) The man saw <u>that there was no one at home</u> when he returned. — Noun clause.
   (d) <u>No one came</u> before the child arrived. — Main clause.
2. witch — wizard; duck — drake; aunt — uncle; vixen — fox; wife — husband. loaves — loaf, armies — army, roofs — roof, sheep — sheep, feet — foot.
3. (1) He sang tunefully;   (5) He chuckled gleefully.
   (2) He frowned angrily.   (6) He smiled broadly.
   (3) He bowed humbly.   (7) He listened attentively.
   (4) He mumbled indistinctly.   (8) He whispered softly
4. a fleet/convoy of ships; a plague of insects; a shoal of herring; a host of angels; a gang of thieves; a pack of wolves; a brood of chickens; a gaggle of geese; a litter of pups; a team of players.
5. *(a)* The house, which was built by Tom's father, was destroyed.
   (b) He works hard at his lesson because he wishes to succeed.
   (c) The men were walking quickly when they saw me.
   (d) As he was passing the church he heard the strains of music.
   (e) The lady lost the book while she was going to the library.

General Tests

TEST 10

1. *(a)* nominative or subjective case; *(b)* a proper noun; *(c)* possessive adjective; *(d)* preposition; *(e)* pastures; *(f)* adverb of time; *(g)* past; *(h)* relative pronoun; *(i)* common; *(j)* adjective.

2. (1) affectionate, natural, attractive, proud, valuable.
   (2) failure, depart, seldom, nonsense, exit.

3. The wood felt coarse to the touch.
   The river followed its course to the sea.
   He tripped over the root of a tree.
   The route was blocked by snow.
   She rode a horse which was as black as night.
   They rowed down the river in their small boat.
   She found a currant in her last piece of cake.
   The strong current swept the bathers out to sea.
   May I borrow your scissors to pare my nails?
   I'm sorry I do not have a pair of scissors.

4. A boy said to his chum, "Where are you going, James?"
   "Oh!" replied the other, "I'm on my way home."

5. *(a)* oasis; *(b)* hermit; *(c)* thermometer; *(d)* optimist; *(e)* tributary.

TEST 11

1. *(a)* I was sure that he would come.
   (b) The watch which he bought was broken when he arrived home.
   (c) He was tired when he reached the station.

2. oxen; tigress; cygnet; igloo; dangerously.

3. Sheep is to Mutton as Pig is to <u>Pork</u>.
   High is to Low as <u>Up</u> is to Down.
   Soldier is to <u>Army</u> as Sailor is to Navy.
   <u>Shoal</u> is to Herring as School is to Whales.
   Bee is to Hive as Cow is to <u>Byre</u>.

4. (1) There is a boy. He is very proud.
   (2) He spoke to me. He was passing.
   (3) The girl gave the right answer. She is intelligent.
   (4) The man bought a boat. It is very big.
   (5) We received word. He was rescued.

General Tests

5. A wet blanket — a discouraging person.
   A rough diamond — an excellent person, though rough mannered.
   A queer fish — an odd person.
   A chip of the old block — very like father.
   To have a bee in one's bonnet — to be obsessed with an idea.
   To bury the hatchet — to make peace.
   To draw the long bow — to tell incredible stories.
   To keep one's powder dry — to be ready, prepared.

TEST 12

1. who — pronoun;   park — noun;   loudly — adverb;   school — adjective; that — conjunction.
   playing — present participle;   bell — objective (or accusative);   boys — plural; subject of heard — boys; they — common gender.

2. (a) lion — masculine; cousin — common; jotter — neuter; waitress — feminine; friend — common.
   (b) lair — den; disappear — vanish; inside — within; empty — vacant; quickly — fast.

3. fruit — greengrocer/fruiterer   spectacles — optician   flowers — florist
   hats — hatter/milliner   milk — dairy   newspapers — newsagent
   fish — fishmonger   meat — butcher   sweets — confectioner
   tobacco — tobacconist

4. (1) The ladies are very beautiful.   (2) Are the salmon fresh?
   (3) The sons-in-law are ill.   (4) The valleys are broad.
   (5) The geese make loud noises.

5. Hoe — gardener;   anvil — blacksmith;   spanner — mechanic;
   solder — tinker/plumber;   palette — artist;   safety-lamp — miner;
   awl — shoemaker/joiner;   "goose" — tailor;   hod — bricklayer;
   cleaver — butcher.

TEST 13

1. (1) William can <u>run</u> faster than <u>I</u>.
   (2) It was <u>I</u> who <u>did</u> it.
   (3) George and <u>he</u> <u>have</u> gone on holiday.
   (4) Between you and <u>me</u> I think they <u>were</u> wrong.
   (5) <u>He</u> and <u>I</u> are twelve years of age.

2. (1) a <u>pack</u> of wolves   (5) a <u>fleet</u> of ships (convoy)
   (2) a <u>swarm</u> of bees   (6) a <u>choir</u> of singers
   (3) a <u>shoal</u> of herring   (7) a <u>gang</u> of thieves
   (4) a <u>herd</u> of cattle   (8) a <u>pack</u> of rascals.

General Tests

3. (1) You ought to visit her now <u>that</u> you know where she stays.
   (2) Write down the answers <u>as</u> you were taught.
   (3) The boy tried hard <u>but</u> he failed.
   (4) <u>When</u> he comes let us know.
   (5) The man was careful <u>lest</u> he should fall.

4. (a) deer, mice, pansies, teeth, women.
   (b) bull, duke, drake, waiter, nephew.

5. A little girl was playing on a busy street.
   Suddenly her ball rolled into the middle of the road, and she ran after it.
   At that moment a motor came dashing round the corner.
   A passer-by saw the girl's danger and ran to her aid.
   Fortunately he saved her from serious injury.

TEST 14

1. (1) How he managed it remains a <u>mystery</u>.
   (2) James was honest and <u>diligent</u>.
   (3) The stranger asked if I could <u>direct</u> him to the station.
   (4) The <u>remedy</u> or cure is very simple.
   (5) His opinion differed <u>from</u> mine.

2. (a) "Tell me," said the old gentleman, "What is your name?"
   (b) reasonable, successful, southern, foolish, French.

3. (1) The bottle was filled <u>with</u> water.
   (2) He was told not to meddle <u>with</u> the toys.
   (3) The two brothers divided the apple <u>between</u> them.
   (4) That hat is similar <u>to</u> mine.
   (5) I hope I can rely <u>on</u> you.

4. (1) rifle — soldier;   (5) letters — postman;
   (2) prescription — chemist/doctor;   (6) pulpit — clergyman;
   (3) telescope — astronomer;   (7) sheep — shepherd;
   (4) spectacles — optician;   (8) joy-stick — aviator/pilot.

5. down in the mouth — <u>in low spirits</u>;   a peppery individual — <u>a cranky person</u>;
   out of sorts — <u>not well</u>;   hard up — <u>short of money</u>;
   beside oneself — <u>overcome with anger or grief</u>

TEST 15

1. (1) glutton; (2) milliner; (3) cousin; (4) cavalry; (5) kennel.

2. present — absent;   bitter — sweet;
   entrance — exit;   polite — impolite;
   east — west;   danger — safety;
   guilty — innocent;   lost — found.

43

General Tests

3. <u>Whom</u> do you think I <u>saw</u>.
   All but one <u>were</u> saved when the ship <u>sank</u>.
   Each of the men <u>has</u> a right to <u>his</u> opinion.
   Between you and <u>me</u> the boys <u>weren't</u> pleased.
   Let you and <u>me</u> stay after the others have <u>gone</u>.

4. as blind as a bat;   as cold as ice;
   as quiet as a mouse;   as good as gold;
   as gentle as a lamb;   as sharp as a needle;
   as happy as a sandboy;   as fresh as a daisy/paint.

5. One day a crow spied a piece of cheese on a window sill.
   She picked it up and flew to a neighbouring tree.
   A cunning fox approached and praised her voice.
   The bird, highly flattered, opened her mouth to sing.
   The cheese fell and was soon eaten by the crafty animal.

SPELLING QUESTIONS
(Answers on page 48)

1. **What is the correct spelling** of the word formed
   (a) When *-ing* is added to these verbs
      appal, offer, prefer, proffer, refer, suffer, kidnap, mimic, worship, admit, limit, equip, gallop.
   (b) When *-ist* is added to these nouns
      journal, medal, novel.
   (c) When *-ous* is added to these nouns
      danger, glamour, humour, marvel.

2. Replace the asterisk in the following words with the missing letter **or letters** of the correct spelling:

   (a) baz*r   ...... a market-place in some Eastern countries.
       bel*ve   ...... to regard as true.
       br*ch   ...... an ornamental clasp.
       cal*nd*r   ...... a table showing months and days in the year.
       campa*n   ...... a series of military operations aimed at an objective.
       cem*t*ry   ...... a place where the dead are buried.
       conc*t   ...... an exaggerated opinion of oneself.
       cricket*r   ...... a person who plays cricket.
       emba*a*ed   ...... disconcerted, perhaps ashamed.
       Feb*ary   ...... the second month of the year.
       f*ld   ...... an enclosed piece of ground.
       forf*t   ...... to lose some right because of a fault.
       fr*nd   ...... a person well-known and liked.
       gove*ment   ...... administration, or a body which administers.
       gr*ve   ...... to sorrow.
       ha*a*ed   ...... troubled, tormented, confused.
       labe*ed   ...... marked with a label.
       l*pard   ...... a spotted animal.
       me*anic   ...... a person skilled in repairing motors.
       misch*v*s   ...... teasing, perhaps harmfully.
       parce*ing   ...... packaging.
       pi*on   ...... a dove.
       rec*t   ...... an acknowledgement of a payment.
       rec*ve   ...... to take into one's possession.
       rec*nise   ...... to identify a known person or thing.
       sec*tary   ...... a person employed to write, type or do other office work.
       s*ve   ...... a strainer for powders or liquids.
       s*ge   ...... an attempt to capture a fortified place by surrounding it.
       s*ze   ...... to grasp, grab.
       trave*er   ...... a person going on a journey.

   (b) access*ble   admiss*ble   defens*ble   imposs*ble   revers*ble
       adapt*ble   collaps*ble   excus*ble   invis*ble
       adjust*ble   contempt*ble feas*ble   reduc*ble

45

Spelling Questions

3. **Spot the difference**

    In addition to distinguishing the similar sounding words found on pages 35 and 36 of *Revised First Aid*, make sure you do not confuse the meanings or spellings of the words listed below. These each lack one letter, **or more**, at the place where the asterisk is printed.

What letter or letters has the asterisk replaced?	Meaning
*ffect (verb)	...... (to) change, influence something or someone.
*ffect (verb)	...... (to) bring about.
*ffect (noun)	...... a result.
alt*r (verb)	...... (to) change.
alt*r (noun)	...... a piece of religious furniture.
as*ent (verb)	...... (to) agree.
as*ent (noun)	...... agreement.
as*ent (noun)	...... a climb.
aug*r (verb)	...... (to) foretell or forebode.
aug*r (noun)	...... an ancient Roman official who interpreted omens or signs.
aug*r (noun)	...... a tool for boring.
br* (verb)	...... (to) shatter.
br* (noun)	...... part of a bicycle or motor-car.
c*ll*r (noun)	...... a piece of clothing for the neck.
c*ll*r (noun)	...... a person paying a visit, or getting in touch by telephone.
compl*ment (verb)	...... (to) complete a required amount.
compl*ment (verb)	...... (to) show respect or admiration.
compl*ment (noun)	...... a remark which shows respect or admiration.
compl*ment (noun)	...... a complete number like that of the crew of a ship.
continu* (adj.)	...... recurring frequently.
continu* (adj.)	...... continuing without a break.
depend*nt (noun)	...... a person who depends on another.
depend*nt (adj.)	...... relying on something or someone.
independ*nt (adj.)	...... not relying on anything or anyone else.
dr*t (noun)	...... a sketch, preliminary drawing or outline of a book or speech.
dr*t (noun)	...... a current of air; quantity of liquid drunk.
dr*t (adj.)	...... a type of beer.
min*r (noun)	...... a man who works in a mine.
min*r (noun)	...... a person under age.
min*r (adj.)	...... less important.

Spelling Questions

mus*(noun)	......	a shellfish.
mus*(noun)	......	flesh which controls body movements by contracting.
sl*(verb)	......	(to) kill.
sl*(noun)	......	a sledge.
station*ry	......	not moving.
station*ry	......	writing materials.
stor*(noun)	......	a tale or narrative.
stor*(noun)	......	a level or tier of a multi-tiered building.

Sentences to Correct

1. I would have liked to have seen that game.
2. Those kind of questions are the most difficult.
3. The police arrested two men who they suspected.
4. You can only stay in the choir if you practice.
5. Your answer is different to mine.
6. We are great friends, him and me.
7. Play quietly, like you said you would.
8. A man who I am sure you know wants to see you.
9. Everyone must behave themselves in this school.
10. You are as smart may be smarter than your brother.
11. He promised he will play today if he has recovered.
12. This typewriter is different than mine.
13. That was a boy whom we knew could do well.
14. They had to reverse back out of the car park.
15. At some schools you can either play rugby or soccer.
16 Wait on me, please. I can't keep up with this bad leg.
17. He will likely be late in the afternoon.
18. No-one is to leave the room until they are finished.
19. Our car is small compared to yours.
20. The present is a joint one for you and I to share.

ANSWERS to Spelling Questions

1. *(a)* appalling, offering, preferring, proffering, referring, suffering, kidnapping, mimicking, worshipping, admitting, limiting, equipping, galloping.

    (b) journalist, medallist, novelist.

    (c) dangerous, glamorous, humorous, marvellous.

2. *(a)* bazaar; believe; brooch; calendar; campaign; cemetery; conceit; cricketer; embarrassed; February; field; forfeit; friend; government; grieve; harassed; labelled; leopard; mechanic; mischievous; parcelling; pigeon; receipt; receive; recognise; secretary; sieve; siege; seize; traveller.

    (b) accessible; adaptable; adjustable; admissible; collapsible; contemptible; defensible; excusable; feasible; impossible; invisible; reducible; reversible.

3. affect/effect/effect; alter/altar; assent/assent/ascent; augur/auger/auger; break/brake; collar/caller; complement/compliment/compliment/complement; continual/continuous; dependant/dependent/independent; draft/draught/draught; miner/minor/minor; mussel/muscle; slay/sleigh; stationary/stationery; story/storey.

Sentences to Correct

1. I should have liked to see that game.
2. That kind of question is the most difficult.
3. The police arrested two men whom they suspected.
4. You can stay in the choir only if you practise.
5. Your answer is different from mine.
6. We are great friends, he and I.
7. Play quietly, as you said you would.
8. A man, whom I am sure you know, wants to see you.
9. Everyone must behave him or herself in this school.
10. You are as smart as, or may be smarter than your brother.
11. He promised he would play today if he had recovered.
12. This typewriter is different from mine.
13. That was a boy who we knew could do well.
14. They had to reverse out of the car park (no back).
15. At some schools you can play either rugby or soccer.
16. Wait for me please. With this bad leg I can't keep up.
17. He will probably be late in the afternoon.
18. No-one is to leave the room until he or she is finished.
19. Our car is small compared with yours.
20. The present is a joint one for you and me to share.